space
and aircraft

© Aladdin Books Ltd 1994

Designed and produced by
Aladdin Books Ltd
28 Percy Street
London W1P 9FF

First published in
the United States in 1994 by
Twenty-First Century Books
A Division of Henry Holt and Company, Inc.
115 West 18th Street
New York, NY 10011

Library of Congress Cataloging–in–Publication Data
Hawkes, Nigel.
      Space and aircraft / Nigel Hawkes. -- 1st ed.
         p. cm. -- (New Technology)
      Includes index.
      ISBN 0-8050-3416-1
      1. Astronautics--Technological innovations--Juvenile literature.
2. Aeronautics--Technological innovations--Juvenile literature.
[1. Astronautics. 2. Aeronautics.] I. Title. II. Series.
TL793.H39 1994
629.4--dc20   94-6717   CIP AC

Design
David West
Children's Book Design
Designers
Steve Woosnam-Savage
Flick Killerby
Editor
Jim Pipe
Picture Research
Brooks Krikler Research
Illustrators
Alex Pang
Ian Thompson

Printed in Belgium

new TECHNOLOGY

space
and aircraft

NIGEL HAWKES

TWENTY-FIRST CENTURY BOOKS
A Division of Henry Holt and Company/New York

CONTENTS

Photocredits
Abbreviations: t-top, m-middle, b-bottom, l-left, r-right
Cover tr, 4, 6-7, 6b: Sikorsky Helicopters; cover bl, 3,
5, 7t, 9t, 22t, 22-23, 24-25 all, 30m: NASA; cover br,
13, 15: Rolls Royce plc; 4t, 8t & 8b, 9b, 27 both:
Science Photo Library; 10-11, 18, 19t, 21 both, 23t &
23b, 26: Frank Spooner Pictures; 10b: Arcana; 11t:
U.S. Air Force; 12-13, 14-15: British Aerospace; 12b,
19b: Virgin Atlantic; 14b, 28b: McDonnell Douglas;
16, 17t: Civil Aviation Authority; 17b: Gulfstream
Aerospace; 28t & 28m: Alitalia; 29: Boeing; 30t:
Mat Irvine.

INTRODUCTION

An amazing variety of aircraft have been developed since man first flew, but in the past 30 years, space technology has pushed the boundaries of flight beyond imagination — higher, faster, and farther, carrying more people to more places. Are there no limits to what can be achieved? This book looks at the very latest developments in aviation and space, some of which are still to make their way from the drawing board into the air, and examines the technology that lies behind them. No branch of engineering makes greater demands or advances more rapidly. The exotic and far-fetched ideas of today are likely to become the commonplaces of tomorrow.

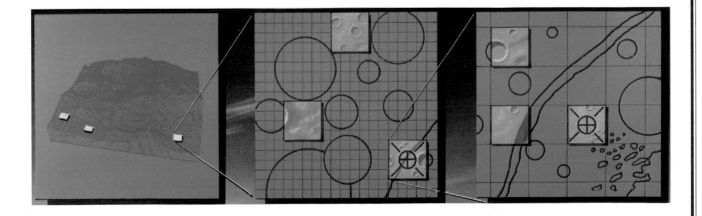

HELICOPTERS
THE NEW BREED

A new breed of helicopter is set to replace fixed-wing aircraft in many applications. Added protection has been given to the tail rotor, which was highly vulnerable in combat and responsible for a quarter of all crashes. Helicopters need this rotor to stop the fuselage from rotating in the opposite way from the main rotor. On the Russian Kamov Ka-50 Werewolf the same result is achieved by the two main rotors spinning in opposite directions, while the McDonnell Douglas Notar blows air past a tail that acts as a vertical wing.

The Boeing/Sikorsky RAH-66 Comanche is designed for armed reconnaissance, attack, and air combat. Very agile, it is harder to detect on radar than existing helicopters. It will also be made largely of composite materials that are lighter than metals. Eight Comanches can be carried in the hold of a C-5 Galaxy transport and can be made flight-ready within 20 minutes of landing.

The Comanche has a tail fan, but to provide protection from damage it is contained inside the tail. The two-man crew will use the latest electronic systems, coupled to a computer, to detect targets from 40 percent greater range. Comanches should also be 40 percent cheaper to operate.

The Comanche can carry a twin-barrel 20 mm cannon, and a choice of three Hellfire or six Stinger missiles in the weapons bays at the sides.

The V-22 Osprey incorporates a more radical design – a tilting wing. It takes off vertically with its engines pointing upward, then swings the wing through 90 degrees, turning into a conventional aircraft. The X-wing (right) is a rotor that can be used for takeoff and then locked in place to act as a fixed wing. Making this concept work is harder than it sounds.

C O M P O S I T E S
S P A C E   A G E   M A T E R I A L S

Composite materials, consisting of glass- and carbon-fiber reinforced plastics, have greatly improved helicopter performance. Extremely strong, they last four times as long as metal. While also used for main frame construction, they make especially good rotor blades, which have always been the most vulnerable part of the helicopter. When the blades are damaged, cracks do not travel through composites as rapidly as through metal, increasing chances of survival. Titanium on the leading edges of the blades ensures a high resistance to erosion.

The rotor blades for the S-61 or Sea King, used in air-sea rescue, consist of plastic resins reinforced by glass or carbon fibers and molded at 250 degrees F. The blade is covered with titanium on the leading edge and glass on the trailing edge.

SPACE PROBES
EXPLORING THE COSMOS

For more than 30 years, unmanned space satellites have explored the solar system. They have filmed the planets from a distance and landed softly on them to search for life. They have probed back into the early history of the universe, using telescopes in orbit beyond the distorting veil of the atmosphere. Since *Mariner 2* – the first satellite to visit another planet – sent back information about Venus in 1962, the Viking spacecraft have landed on Mars, and the former Soviet Union has explored Venus. In addition, the two Voyager spacecraft have conducted a grand tour of the outer planets before disappearing into the immensity of interstellar space. Of the planets in our solar system, only distant Pluto remains unexplored. At far less cost than manned missions, space probes can provide vast amounts of information, and go to places humans will never visit.

Not all space probes work perfectly; some disappointments are inevitable because if something goes wrong in space there is little chance of fixing it. *Mars Observer* was launched to provide data needed for a more detailed exploration of the planet, and eventually for a manned mission. Unfortunately, it failed on the last lap without sending any data. The space scientists had to start again.

Mars Observer, *launched in 1992, was supposed to map the planet from orbit, but blew up just as it was going into orbit, probably due to a fuel leak.*

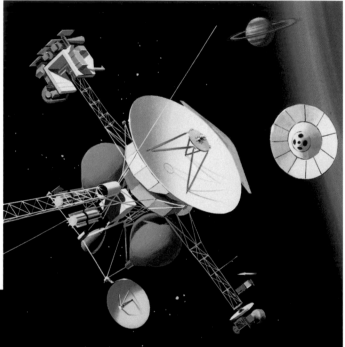

The Cassini *satellite, due for launch in 1996, is designed to explore Titan, the largest of Saturn's moons. To get there, Cassini will use the gravity of the earth and Jupiter to gain speed, passing the earth in 1998 and Jupiter in 2000 before arriving at Saturn in 2002. When it reaches Saturn, it will send a probe down into Titan's atmosphere, and fly by two more moons, Iapetus and Enceladus.*

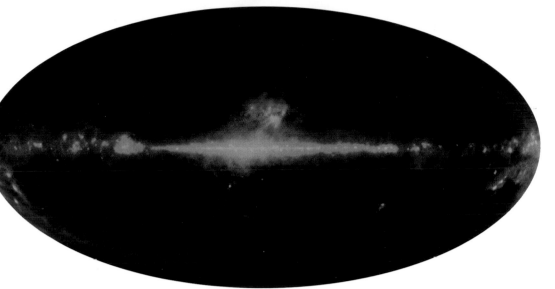

Data gathered by the COBE satellite at infrared wavelengths shows that radiation is unevenly spread across the sky. The plane of the Milky Way – our galaxy – lies across the middle of the image. If the images had shown a perfectly smooth spread of infrared, the COBE satellite would have disproved the theory that stars and planets grew from concentrations of dust created by the Big Bang.

The COBE satellite has an antenna tuned to radiation emitted billions of years ago when the universe had only just begun. COBE's findings provided firm evidence that the universe did start with a Big Bang.

Cosmologists believed in a theory called the "Big Bang," but couldn't prove it. Their theory stated that the universe started with an incredible explosion, sending particles out in all directions. Some particles joined together in small clouds of dust that eventually turned into stars and planets. In order to study these events, which happened billions of years ago, they designed the Cosmic Background Explorer, or COBE, to look at the band of radiation emitted when the universe was still a hot fireball.

AIRPOWER
STRIVING FOR STEALTH

Exotic shapes and sophisticated new electronic systems have created a generation of planes invisible to radar. The experience of surface-to-air missiles in wars in the Middle East and Vietnam convinced strategists that in future aircraft would have to elude detection by radar and attack by heat-seeking missiles. The first practical stealth war planes emerged in the 1991 Gulf War – the U.S. B-2 stealth bomber and the F-117A stealth fighter. Stealth technology means making an aircraft hard to detect in every way: by radar, by sight, by sound, or by the heat of its engines.

The engines of a conventional bomber give off a huge amount of heat in producing their 75 megawatts of power, while a modern infrared detector is sensitive enough to track a lighted cigarette at 30 miles. To make the engines of the B-2 less obvious to the detectors, they are designed to be quiet and cool, and are tucked away in the base of the wings. On the F-117A fighter, known to pilots as the "Wobbly Goblin," the two engines are buried in the thick inner portion of the wings. The fuselage and wing are designed as one because the wing root, where wing and fuselage join, can create a very strong radar echo.

(Below) The Aurora – this reconstruction is what some people think the mystery plane looks like. If it exists, it would be able to fly very high, very fast, and for thousands of miles without refueling on reconnaissance missions over enemy territory.

U.S.A.F

The Northrop B-2 bomber, which first flew in 1989, looks as if it is all wing and no plane. The smooth shape reduces radar echoes by minimizing sharp angles and vertical surfaces. For the same reason, the B-2 has no fin. This would normally make it impossible to fly, so computerized fly-by-wire techniques are used to keep it under control. The B-2 also has complex electronic systems for confusing the enemy, and special paints and materials for a lower radar signature.

CODE NAME AURORA
A HIGH-FLYING MYSTERY

Perhaps surprisingly, no order has been placed for a type of aircraft where stealth is most important of all, the high-flying surveillance aircraft. This has not prevented people from speculating that such an aircraft is being built in secret, under the code name Aurora (see far left), and occasional sightings of the aircraft over Scotland have fed the rumors. Although aircraft have been developed in secret before, concealing an advanced aircraft like Aurora for so long would be a major achievement. However, disappointingly, it looks as if Aurora is just a fantasy.

The Lockheed F-117A (above left) does have a tail, but not a vertical one. Its two fins form a V-shape, reducing radar echo. The angles and facets of the plane reflect light and radar in every direction like a cut jewel, confusing defenders. To reduce heat, the two General Electric turbofan engines are deeply buried and not fitted with afterburners, though this does mean a big loss of power.

Incoming radar signals bounce off the panels of the F-117A in every direction. This means that there is no single strong echo bouncing back to give the aircraft's position away. It merges into the background.

11

MEGA-JETS

THE BIGGEST JUMBOS YET

By the first years of the new millenium, huge new planes that will dwarf today's jumbo jets will be dominating the skies. The most successful of the current jumbos, the Boeing 747, can carry 400 or more passengers up to 8,000 miles, but the next generation of mega-jets will have room for 800 or even 1,000 people. This is 40 times bigger than the world's first really successful airliner, the Douglas DC3 of 1936. There may be a problem finding space in today's airports for the huge planes. However, the growth of air traffic is expected to double to two billion passengers a year by 2005, and airports and air-traffic control systems are already at full stretch. To carry more people, the airlines need bigger planes – Boeing, Airbus, and McDonnell Douglas already have designs on the drawing board. No major breakthroughs are needed to get these "super-jumbos" airborne: the materials to make them and the engines to power them already exist.

One of the greatest problems with the new planes will be ensuring that the powerful wake they create does not disturb aircraft flying close behind them. At worst, this could mean such large delays between planes during takeoff and landing that much of the advantage of the mega-jets would be lost. Another problem will be maneuvering aircraft on the ground, and in some smaller airports folding or telescopic wings may be required.

Boeing's super-jumbo design (above) looks a lot like the familiar 747: four engines and a fat, round body. But it would be much bigger, and 180 tons heavier than the 747.

***The worst thing about** long flights is the lack of space. Mega-jets may have room for self-service restaurants and space for passengers to stretch their legs. They will certainly have video consoles and phones for in-flight calls fitted to every seat. Experienced travelers treat such claims with scepticism as the more people the airlines can squeeze on a flight, the greater their profit.*

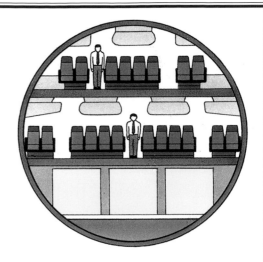

Airbus envisages a triple-decker aircraft (right) with an egg-shaped cross section. Economy class will be in the top deck, business class in the middle, and first class in the lower deck, which will include beds. Boeing's more traditional design for up to 800 passengers (far right), is circular. The top two decks run the full length of the plane and the lowest deck is reserved for luggage.

To create the new mega-jets, the simplest option might be to stretch the 747 even farther than the 600-seat 747-400X has done, by adding sections that take advantage of the new wing design. The European consortium Airbus has another design for a fuselage consisting of two tubes side by side, known as the "double-bubble." Building such big planes will be so expensive that no single company is likely to have the resources.

MEGA-JET ENGINES
POWER & ECONOMY

Engines powerful enough for the mega-jets are already available. The Rolls-Royce Trent 800, fitted to the twin-engined Boeing 777, produces 39 tons of thrust and gulps in more than a ton of air every second – enough to empty a cathedral-sized space in less than a minute. Big engines like the Trent have been built to ensure that today's twin-engined planes, increasingly common even on long-distance flights, can still fly safely even if one engine fails. The Trent is economical as well as powerful: at 600 mph, it consumes no more fuel per passenger mile than a car at 60 mph. This is twice as efficient as the engines in the 1960s.

SUPERSONICS

PAST THE SOUND BARRIER

So far, only two supersonic airliners have ever flown in commercial service. While the Soviet TU-144 had a brief and unsuccessful career, the Anglo-French Concorde has proved popular and reliable, though only 16 have been built. The problems of supersonic airliners are many. The airframe gets hot, so aluminum alloys cannot be used but have to be replaced by more expensive and heavier titanium or stainless steel. The fuselage must be slender, making the cabin narrow. Producing engines that are powerful enough yet acceptably quiet is also difficult. The scientific efficiency of a supersonic transport, expressed as the ratio between lift and drag, is much lower than for a subsonic plane. However, this is offset by the extra comfort of the SST because it spends less time in the air as a result of its greater speed.

Several aerospace companies have produced designs for the next generation of SSTs. NASA is working with Boeing and McDonnell Douglas, and the engine makers Pratt & Whitney and General Electric, to discover if it is possible to produce an SST that will operate at a profit. In Europe, a consortium of plane manufacturers has produced plans for the so-called "son of Concorde," a 250-seat SST with a range of 6,000 miles and a speed of 1,400 mph. But all SSTs will still have to satisfy concerns about noise pollution – a worry because they fly so much higher than subsonics – and the sonic boom, which has kept Concorde from flying supersonic over land.

This British Aerospace design (right) takes into account lessons learned from Concorde.

The McDonnell Douglas design for a commercial SST is a 300-passenger plane capable of Mach 2 (twice the speed of sound) and with a range of 5,000 nautical miles. The wing, like most of the new SST designs, is of the "cranked arrow" form, with a pronounced kink in the leading edge. This shape offers a considerable improvement in efficiency.

SSTs have slender, arrow-shaped fuselages, which must retain their strength when heated by supersonic flight. They also need great rigidity, to resist higher pressurization. As a result, weight per seat in Concorde is three times that of a Boeing 747.

(Above right) This development by Rolls-Royce employs a special air intake system for the additional airflow into the engine at subsonic speeds.

SST POWERHOUSE
EFFICIENCY AT ALL SPEEDS

SST engines must combine quietness and power at low speeds with the ability to deliver high velocities when cruising. This can be achieved by designing an engine with variable nozzles. These allow much more air to pass through the engine at low speeds than at high speeds. In the mid tandem fan, doors at the front of the engine open and close.

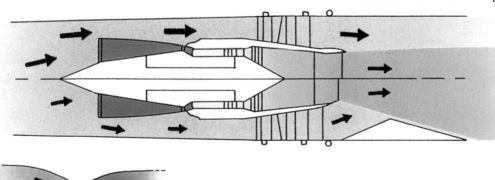

SAFER SKIES

AIR TRAFFIC CONTROL

Europe's skies are in danger of being clogged up with passenger aircraft. More than 2,500 flights a year are held up by an average of 22 minutes because the air-traffic control systems cannot cope with the volume of traffic. Luckily, help is on the way: a new generation of computer-controlled systems should ease congestion soon. Satellites will provide exact positions for every aircraft, and improve communications by allowing computer data to be sent direct to the aircraft cockpit showing which course to fly and any aircraft nearby. On a screen in the control tower the position, course and speed of every aircraft will be registered automatically. Planes take off along six fixed tracks, with six more tracks for landing. Using this system, aircraft will fly closer together but safely. Landing in low visibility should also be easier.

The American global positioning-satellite network will be used to pinpoint the position of each aircraft to within about 100 feet. A Russian satellite network will be used for communication, sending instructions to a screen in the cockpit. The system will be quicker and less error-prone than voice communication.

(Left) At the heart of the air-traffic control system is the tower. Today visual observation of the aircraft is less important than it used to be, thanks to radar and other aids, but airports usually retain towers. Yet in spite of all the improvements in computers, it is unlikely that human controllers will be replaced. For quick decisions in difficult circumstances, there is nothing to beat an experienced human brain.

(Right) Air-traffic controllers use strips of paper that have all the data on each plane, modifying them as the flight proceeds. In future these details will appear on the controller's screen. Computers will track planes 20 minutes ahead.

COLLISION ALERT
TRAFFIC CONTROL SYSTEMS

On board each aircraft, a display panel controlled by computers will show pilots where any nearby aircraft are (below). If they come too close, threatening a collision or a near miss, a Traffic Alert and Collision Avoidance System will tell each pilot what evasive action to take. Near misses are fairly rare but increasing air traffic will need tighter controls.

Pilots landing on instruments fly down a narrow beam of radio waves, which tells them whether they are at the right height and heading. In the future, these will be replaced by a wide cone of microwaves that allow curved approaches to be made even in the foggiest conditions.

BALLOONS

CARRIERS FOR A NEW AGE

The first flights were made in balloons, lifted by hot air or by hydrogen gas. Lighter-than-air machines like these were once seen as the liners of the skies, sailing serenely around the world while the passengers relaxed in spacious lounges. In the 1930s the disastrous crashes of the British *R101* and the German *Hindenberg* put an end to that dream, ironically just as a safe gas had been found. However, in the past few years new technology has given fresh life to balloons as an exciting sports challenge and even as cargo carriers. Both the Atlantic and the Pacific have successfully been crossed by helium-filled and hot-air balloons, using the jet stream winds that blow around the earth at a height of 20,000 feet and at speeds of up to 200 mph. The final challenge is to fly all the way around the world without stopping.

A unique double-balloon has been designed to attempt the trip. A pressurized capsule big enough for a crew of three is lifted by a helium balloon, while below it hangs a second balloon filled with air serving as ballast. At night when it is cold, the helium gives less lift, so air is bled off. By day a compressor refills the ballast balloon.

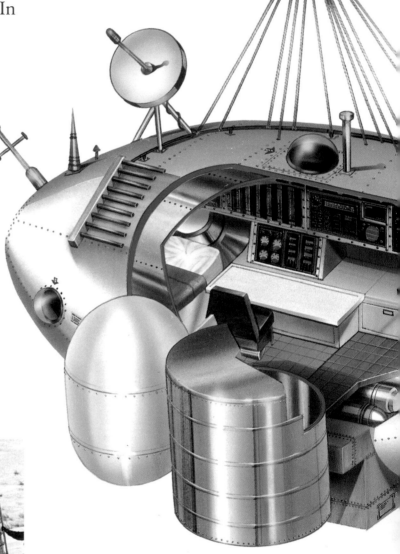

(Left) The Earthwinds Hilton *capsule lies on the ground in Nevada, surrounded by canopy material, after an unsuccessful attempt to take off on the around-the-world trip. Launching the complex balloon is the trickiest part of the mission, possible only when weather conditions are perfect. This problem has delayed the trip for several years.*

The Russian dirigible designed by the Moscow Aeronautical Institute is the latest attempt to revive the airship. The Rossia is a disk-shaped rigid balloon more than 600 feet across and 200 feet high. Designed to lift and transport 600 ton cargoes to out-of-the-way places, the Rossia can cruise at about 100 mph at a maximum altitude of 1,500 feet. Its range without refueling is nearly 3,000 miles.

РОССИЯ 4001

The crew of the Earthwinds Hilton balloon will live in a 24-foot pressurized capsule made of glass fiber-reinforced plastic. A single bunk will enable them to take turns to rest. Fuel and liquid helium tanks are strapped to the outside. On the trip, expected to take 14 days, the crew will be in regular touch with base, and even carry a fax machine so that a daily newspaper can be faxed to them.

Dirigibles are balloons with a rigid frame and propellers that allow them to be steered. They use inert helium rather than hydrogen and can reach speeds of 100 mph or so. They are ideal for aerial observation or photography. New lightweight materials for the framework and canopy (below right) have convinced some people that dirigibles have a future as cargo carriers.

A BRAVE ATTEMPT
THE VIRGIN ATLANTIC CROSSING

The first crossing of the Atlantic by hot-air balloon was made by Richard Branson and Per Lindstrand in the Virgin *Atlantic Flyer* in 1987. The huge balloon, made by the British company Thunder & Colt, had a capacity of over two million cubic feet. The top of the balloon consisted of nylon with shiny aluminized Melinex film on both sides, designed to catch the heat of the sun and save on fuel. The lower part of the canopy, where the burners feed in hot air, was protected by black fire-resistant fabric. The trip almost ended in disaster when the balloon crashed in the Irish Sea, and Lindstrand jumped out. Branson then took off again, before descending and bailing out. Luckily, both men were picked up unhurt by the Royal Navy.

SPACE PLANES

TRAVELING AT MACH 18

Beyond the supersonic transport lies a new kind of plane altogether, one that combines flight and space technology to reach speeds of more than 10,000 mph.

The German space-plane design, Sanger, consists of a rocket piggy-backing on a hypersonic aircraft. The mother craft would carry the second stage rocket high into the atmosphere and up to a speed of Mach 16, where it would separate and go into orbit. The British version, called Hotol, has been developed by British Aerospace and Rolls-Royce.

These craft would have two jobs: getting satellites into space far more cheaply than shuttles or rockets can, and serving as passenger aircraft capable of getting to the other end of the earth in an hour or so. They would need new engines, and new heat-resistant materials for the fuselage. One idea used on the American National Aerospace Plane (NASP) is the scramjet, a jet engine that uses the speed of the plane through the air to ram air into the combustors, where it mixes with fuel and burns.

NASP would use liquid hydrogen as fuel for its scramjet engines. The hydrogen would be piped to the leading edges of the wings as a coolant. The main structure would be of titanium, but ceramics would be needed at the nose, where temperatures would reach 4,900 degrees F.

Turbojet

Scramjet

Space planes will need two types of engines. In this early NASA design (left), an ordinary turbo-jet engine is used for takeoff from the runway and acceleration to 2,000 mph. At this speed, scramjets can take over because the airflow is sufficiently fast for them to work. Scramjets could not be used alone, because they only begin operating effectively at high speeds.

The NASP X-30 is intended to be a major element of the United States' planned permanently manned orbital space station, called Freedom.

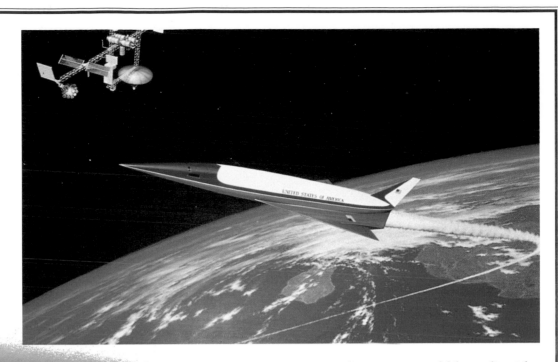

Hotol's engine would burn liquid hydrogen and oxygen from the atmosphere to get it to high speed. Only as the air thins would it need to start burning the liquid oxygen carried on board. As a result, Hotol should be able to transport twice as much cargo as a shuttle.

Liquid hydrogen   Liquid oxygen

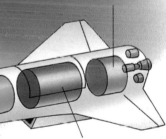

Payload

High-temperature insulation

Tank wall

Expansion

Most of the space inside Hotol would consist of a tank of liquid hydrogen. The tank walls would form part of the space plane's structure, linked directly to its outer skin (right). High-temperature insulation would be needed to keep the fuel tank cool. In wind tunnels, the Hotol design has been tested at speeds up to Mach 18 – the expected reentry speed.

The space shuttle uses five main engines to reach orbit: three rocket engines on the shuttle orbiter, and two solid-fuel boosters. Once in orbit, it has two smaller orbital engines, together with 44 jet thrusters, for maneuvering. The solid-fuel boosters separate before orbit, and parachute into the sea, from which they can be recovered for reuse. The cargo bay is huge (about the size of a railroad car) and is used for carrying satellites and other equipment into earth orbit.

THE SHUTTLE

A REUSABLE ROCKET

Once used, conventional rocket engines and fuel tanks are cast adrift in space. The space shuttle was designed to make the process of getting into space much cheaper by using the same vehicle again and again. Taking off like a rocket from a launchpad, the shuttle can go into orbit, then return to reenter the atmosphere and glide to a landing on a conventional runway. Refurbished and refueled, it is ready for another flight. However, the idea that it would be a lot cheaper than rockets has proved false. Though the U.S. shuttle program was set back by the destruction of the shuttle *Challenger* in 1986, with the loss of all seven crew members, over 40 flights have now been completed since the first in 1981.

Three main rocket engines burning hydrogen and oxygen provide power for launch. Two smaller orbital engines are used to slow the shuttle down for reentry into the atmosphere. The rocket engines have been very reliable.

The cavernous payload bay of the shuttle can carry satellites or space laboratories such as the European-made Spacelab into orbit. A long articulated arm lifts the satellites from the bay and releases them into orbit.

Flying the shuttle has turned out to be far more expensive than expected. Because it is a manned system, it must carry life-support systems and be designed to high safety standards, unlike an unmanned mission. It takes much longer than expected to turn the shuttle around between flights, leading to fewer flights and a greater cost for each one. The shuttle does have advantages. Astronauts can be sent up to repair satellites in orbit, and the shuttle can fetch as well as carry, collecting satellites from orbit and returning them to earth if needed. Other countries also have looked at space shuttles – below is an artist's impression of a project by the Japanese National Space Development Agency (NASDA).

The living area of the shuttle is on two levels, with the flight deck above. The crew sleep in the mid-deck below, where there is a toilet, galley, and the airlock for getting into the unpressurized payload bay.

(Below) The NASDA H-II Orbiting plane, or "HOPE," would use a booster rocket to lift it to low-earth orbit. An unmanned spacecraft, HOPE would lift and retrieve satellites and experiments from space, returning to earth after 100 hours.

The shuttle glides in to land without power, and at high speeds of about 200 mph. This means that the flight crew has no chance to go around again if they make a mistake on the approach. Special ceramic tiles on the underside and the nose resist the heat of reentry.

PLANET MARS

A FUTURE COLONY?

Of all the planets in the solar system, only Mars provides a possible alternative to the earth as a place to live. The other planets are either too cold, too hot, too distant, or too insubstantial (consisting of clouds of gas) to contemplate settling there. Even Mars is inhospitable, with little oxygen, virtually no water, and night temperatures of -58 degrees F. Winds blowing at 100 mph sweep across its surface, whipping up dust storms. The first manned mission is still many years off, but a series of unmanned missions in the next few years will pave the way. Russian scientists plan two missions, in 1994 and 1996, which will place landers on the Martian surface along with the six-wheeled vehicle *Marsokhod,* which will wander across the planet. On the 1996 mission, a French-designed hot-air balloon will be released. By day, the heat of the sun will heat the gas in the balloon, causing it to drift across the Martian surface, while at night it will descend to the ground to make soil analyses. The United States has also planned to place 16 landers on Mars between 1999 and 2003, in a program called the Mars Environmental Survey.

(Below) Approaching Mars: this is what a Mars transporter might look like, firing its banks of ion thrusters as it goes into a circular orbit around the planet. Assembled in earth orbit, the huge nuclear-powered vehicle could carry 130-ton loads to Mars in six and a half months, doing a complete round trip every four years.

(Left) A Mars lander leaves earth orbit on top of a 33-foot diameter nuclear-powered rocket. Each nuclear engine can produce 25,000 pounds of thrust. Such rockets, driven by small nuclear reactors, are the only power sources believed capable of the journey to Mars.

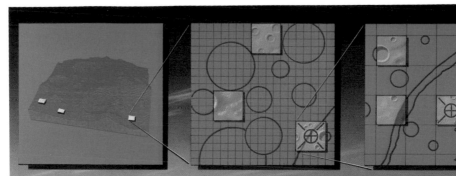

Robotic spacecraft with their own vision system will land on Mars long before humans do. As they get near the ground the resolution of their visual system increases, as this series of images shows. They then pick the safest spot to land.

A manned mission to Mars will be a lot more complex, almost certainly requiring the space vehicle to be assembled in earth orbit before setting off. A cargo vehicle would set off first, to make a soft landing on the planet carrying food, fuel, and materials. Once that had landed safely the manned mission would set off. The round trip might take a year, with two to three weeks spent on the Martian surface.

(Right) The first human mission to Mars, around the year 2019, may look like this. Astronauts take measurements while their lander waits to take them back to a station in Mars orbit.

TELESCOPES

AVOIDING ARMAGEDDON

Scientists believe that when dinosaurs became extinct, about sixty-five million years ago, it was probably the result of an asteroid or comet about six miles across smashing into the earth.

The dust thrown up by the explosion blotted out the sun, altering the climate, and over thousands of years the dinosaurs gradually died out. Today some astronomers fear history may repeat itself. If one of the bigger asteroids collided with the earth, the results could be cataclysmic. So, in addition to using their telescopes to explore the cosmos, astronomers have now trained them on incoming objects to calculate their orbits precisely, so that collisions can be predicted. Already they have found there are many more near-misses than they had realized: in 1990 a small object came within 100,000 miles of the earth, only half the distance to the moon. The next step will be to work out how to deflect such devastating objects.

Nuclear weapons might be used to break up incoming asteroids. Alternatively, the heat of the sun could be focused by mirrors in space to direct an intense beam on the asteroid (below). The surface would be heated to between 1,800° F and 3,600° F, vaporizing it and producing a jet of material that would alter the asteroid's course enough to make it miss the earth.

(Above) The world's biggest radio-telescope has been built in a natural hollow in Puerto Rico.

(Above and left) The Keck telescope, opened in 1992 in Hawaii, is the world's biggest. In the background picture, a long exposure shows the stars as circular streaks across the sky, while the above picture shows the open dome of the telescope from the top. To spot asteroids, a telescope as big as the Keck is not really needed, but it will help astronomers puzzle out the mysteries of the cosmos.

CHRONOLOGY

The Wright brother's Flyer I

EARLY PLANES

1903 The most important date in flying went almost unnoticed. On December 17, 1903, Wilbur and Orville Wright made the first powered flights in a heavier-than-air machine at Kitty Hawk, North Carolina. Wilbur, in the last flight of the day, stayed aloft for nearly a minute and covered 284 yards.

1905 In their third aircraft, the Flyer III, Wilbur flew over 25 miles in 39 minutes. But the Wrights were secretive men who demanded firm orders before they would reveal their secrets; so few believed them.

1906 The year of the first flight to take place in Europe, made by the Frenchman Albert Santos-Dumont.

1907 Henri Farman, an Englishman living in France, flew more than two-thirds of a mile.

1908 The Wrights took Flyer III to Europe and on September 21 Wilbur made a flight of 41 miles, staying up for an hour and a half, and setting an altitude record of 360 feet.

1909 Frenchman Louis Bleriot flew the English Channel.

1919 John Alcock and Arthur Whitten Brown flew the Atlantic in their Vickers Vimy.

1927 Charles Lindbergh became a hero by flying the Atlantic alone, in the Spirit of St Louis.

EARLY AIRLINERS

1919 The first daily passenger service by air, using five-seater AEG biplanes, was between Berlin and Weimar.

1926 The first successful airliner was the Ford Trimotor, which by 1929 was regularly crossing the U.S. coast-to-coast in 48 hours.

1936 Air travel was revolutionized by the Douglas DC3, an all-metal twin-engined airliner with 21 seats.

1939 Boeing's Type 13 flying boat could cruise for 3,500 miles at a speed of 170 mph.

The Graf Zeppelin *crossed the Atlantic over 144 times*

AIRSHIPS

1783 The Montgolfier brothers made the first manned flight in a hot air balloon.

1900 The first Zeppelin airship flew in Germany. Designed by Count Ferdinand von Zeppelin, a cavalry officer, it was 420 feet long.

1928 The most successful airship ever, the Graf Zeppelin, flew over a million miles.

1930 Britain's attempt to match the German Zeppelins ended when R101 crashed on its maiden flight to India.

1937 The first airship era ended when the giant Hindenberg burst into flames in New Jersey, killing 36.

A Douglas DC3 operated by Alitalia

JET PLANES
1939 The first jet aircraft to fly was the He-178, powered by an engine designed by Dr. Hans Joachim von Ohain.

SUPERSONIC PLANES
1947 The first supersonic flight was made on October 14 by Charles "Chuck" Yeager in the U.S. rocket plane Bell X-1.

The Stratocruiser had the first pressurized cabin.

HELICOPTERS
1936 The first practical helicopter was developed by Heinrich Focke, who had been a German pilot in World War I. His Fa-61, flown by Ewald Rolfs, hovered for 15 minutes.

1939 Igor Sikorsky, a Russian-born inventor, flew the first single-rotor helicopter, the VS-300 (above). By 1941, Sikorsky had mastered the art of controlling the helicopter and regularly put on flying shows, always wearing a Fedora hat. On May 6, 1941 he stayed up for more than an hour and a half.

1941 Britain's first jet, the Gloster/Whittle E.28/39, flew for the first time. Its engine was the work of Frank Whittle.

1948 The F-86 Sabre was the first combat aircraft to exceed the speed of sound.

A V-2 Rocket

ROCKETS
1400 The first rockets were made by the Chinese, as weapons of war.

1806 Rockets were used against Napoleon, but they lacked accuracy.

1926 American engineer Robert Goddard launched the first liquid-fueled rocket.

1932 In Nazi Germany, Wernher von Braun launched a successful liquid-fueled rocket, and began a program of research which he was to continue after the war, for the United States' Government.

1944 On September 8, three people were killed in London, the first victims of von Braun's V-2. By the end of the war, 1,403 V-2s had been fired at London.

1962 The X-15 rocket plane holds the altitude record for an airplane, having reached a height of 67 miles. It flew at five times the speed of sound.

1952 The world's first jet airliner, the Comet 1, started flights from London to Johannesburg.

1958 The Boeing 707 went into service as the first reliable jet airliner.

1969 First flight of the Boeing 747, the only real jumbo jet so far and still dominating the skies today.

1968 The Soviet Union was the first to test a supersonic transport, the Tu-144. However, it never served as a passenger plane outside Soviet territory and is now discontinued.

1969 The first successful supersonic transport aircraft, Concorde, made its maiden flight.

The A-1 Sputnik rocket

29

SPACE ROCKETS

1957 Building on German work, the Soviet Union had by 1957 produced a rocket with a range of 4,000 miles. On October 4, the space age began with the launch of Sputnik 1, a tiny satellite with a radio transmitter that emitted a series of beeps.

1958 America's first satellite, Explorer 1, was launched by Von Braun on a Redstone rocket.

1961 The first man in space Yuri Gagarin, was launched in his Vostock capsule on April 12.

1962 John Glenn made three orbits of the earth in Friendship 7.

1969 The first manned landing on the moon was achieved by the U.S., which had by now overtaken the Soviet lead in manned space flights. Neil Armstrong and Buzz Aldrin set foot on the moon on July 21: "One small step for man, one giant leap for mankind."

SPACE PROBES

1962 The first American unmanned space probe, Ranger 4, reached the moon. In the same year the U.S. Orbiting Solar Laboratory made the first astronomical observations in space.

1965 The U.S. Mariner 4 photographed Mars.

1976 A Viking probe landed on Mars.

1977 Voyagers 1 and 2 launched by the U.S. on a grand tour of the outer planets. They are now at the edge of the solar system, about to leave it.

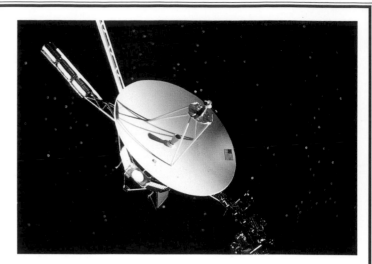

The probe Voyager 2

A Space Shuttle

F-117A stealth fighter

1983 Pioneer 10, an American probe, became the first man-made object to travel beyond the planets.

1985 Ariane launched the Giotto probe which successfully tracked Halley's Comet.

1990 The Hubble space telescope was put into earth orbit by the shuttle.

1992 COBE discovered patterns of radiation that seemed to confirm the Big Bang theory of how the stars and planets had formed.

SHUTTLES

1981 First launch of the U.S. shuttle, designed to be a cheaper form of space transport.

1986 The shuttle Challenger blew up, killing all on board.

1988 The Soviet shuttle Buran (Snowstorm) had its one and only flight.

GLOSSARY

Afterburner
Device for providing more power in a jet by burning fuel in the exhaust gases.

Composite
Material made by combining two or more distinct substances so as to take advantage of their properties.

Dirigible
Balloon with a rigid internal frame, and engines driving propellers to move it. Unlike a hot air balloon, it can be steered.

Drag
Force exerted by the air when an object travels through it, slowing it down.

Fly-by-wire
Technique whereby the pilot's movements are conveyed to the control surfaces of an aircraft by computer signals sent to hydraulic motors. This means that pilots do not have to rely on their own strength to pull the aircraft straight in certain difficult situations.

Infrared
Light that lies just outside the visible region of the spectrum; it cannot be detected by the eye but can be picked up by instruments or sensitive film.

Mach number
Measure of speed, named after the Czechoslovakian physicist, Ernst Mach. Mach 1 is the speed of sound, Mach 2 twice the speed of sound, and so on.

Microwaves
Radiation of wavelengths between infrared and radio waves; used in air-traffic control and in microwave ovens.

Nuclear engine
Rocket engine that gets its power from a nuclear reactor.

Radar signature
Characteristic echo created by any solid object picked up by radar. The signature depends on the shape and structure of an object.

Sonic boom
A loud explosive sound caused by the shock wave of an aircraft that travels faster than the speed of sound.

Stealth technology
Method of reducing the radar and infrared signature of an aircraft or ship so as to reduce the chance that it will be detected.

Supersonic
Able to travel faster than the speed of sound, which at sea level is 743 mph.

Turbofan
Jet engine in which a large part of the air is sucked around rather than through the engine.

INDEX